Our Body
and
our Flesh

*

essay

*

Traumear

*

This difficult but important contemporary didactic work
replies to the following five questions:

1. What is our body
   and how can we make use of it?
2. Why and how are we tempted
   to make insufficient use of it?
3. How does our body compare to our flesh?
4. How do we use or abuse our body
   and can we own our flesh?
5. How does carnal pain relate to our flesh?

* * *

Our Body and our Flesh

Our body is such that if we make no use, or insufficient use, of it, it registers abuse. This abuse, which we are then forced to notice as pain, is carnal in character. Some questions such as the following therefore need to be answered:

1. What is our body and how can we make use of it?
2. Why and how are we tempted to make insufficient use   of it?
3. How does our body compare to our flesh?
4. How do we use or abuse our body an can we own our flesh?
5. How does carnal pain relate to our flesh?

1
What is our body and how can we make use of it?

From the beginning it might be wise to call to mind that when we refer to our body we do not mean something that can be used or not used. If it is in fact our body, live and concrete, it cannot be other than in use. To the extent that it is not in use it is not our body. We mean something somewhat different when we speak of 'the human body', because that is mythic. It is not a myth but mythic. 'Our' body, which is owned by us, does not have to be described as human because it cannot be other than human. Human beings are more or less in possession of their bodies. Another, perhaps more difficult consideration is the following: Not humanity, nor human being as such, implies possession of bodily attributes but being a human being does. We have to be willing to think our way through various levels of definition here.

Conventionally we are taught, and taught to believe, that our bodies are flesh and blood. Bodily attributes and carnality are supposed to overlap if not to coincide or even to amount to the same. This is not true; however we have to be careful, because the opposite is not true either.

Let's dive into the deep end here and state that when we see, and equally when we hear, taste, touch and smell, and when we do this in such a way that it can be said to be done in truth, we possess our body, at least to that degree, in use. (We will not go into the topic: What is truth? but rather deal truthfully with whatever we touch on, so that the answer to 'what is truth?' will be self-evident, rather like the open secret J.W. Goethe mentions.) Still further degrees of body ownership are available to us by way of feeling, emotion and passion. None of these exist in isolation, of course. One can never be quite sure nowadays what all needs to be mentioned because these are transitional times in our western cultural neck of the woods, so that the same word can have a great variety of connotations depending on who uses it. For my own peace of mind I like to use the word 'vision' as a collective term for the five senses, though not exclusively.

While cautioning against the bad habit of picturing human faculties in isolation, I should perhaps extend that caution to the physical realm, in which 'mind' and 'body' occur actively as our mind and our body in union. The implication here is that our body can never be other than in union with our mind, again at least to a degree. Being intellectual, like being emotional, is not a physical attribute and therefore neither can we say that our body or mind are involved. We talk about intellectuals. No reason why we should no also refer to 'emotionals', except that not so many are around. Our culture for a long time has been mind-heavy and body-poor. We should be more concerned about mental hypertrophy but eastern cultures have equal cause to be concerned over body-hypertrophy. Separate passion is no less immature than separate conception.

So the body we own, and therefore the truthful seeing and feeling we are able to do, may be viewed on its own, distinct from our mind, but never in separation from it. Our reason and purpose, after all, for viewing it is perhaps to bring it up to par but finally we actually want to use it. So we might look at each side of a coin, to ascertain the genuineness of the coin, but then our main aim is not to admire it but to spend it. I like to think of our body and our mind as face and obverse of our soul. Again, this does not mean that we cannot be aware of our soul in itself and as a whole. After all a penny is not made up of its two sides.

I don't see why we cannot continue to use the metaphor of the penny when we consider ourselves as sliding into popularity. Now it's not the penny we look at and spend but the penny before it is made. As popular, rather than human, beings we 'see' ourselves through other eyes, the eyes of society or of our family for example and our purpose is not to become whole but to be partial. So here we have something like copper for the penny, and molds, or whatever they are called, for impressing the slug, but we have no intention of creating a usable coin.

The question 'what is our body' is difficult to answer only to the extent that we try to do so using language conventional for the purpose of describing 'the human body' which in turn is 'seen' as a multitude of carnal responses and reactions. First of all, the human body is no such thing and secondly our body is not the human body.

I know that initially I asked the question: What is our body and how can we make use of it? We can see now how the question is misleading to start with. What about the question: What is your arm and how can you connect it to your shoulder? Does that make sense? Only to a surgeon, who deals with 'body parts'. We have a different agenda. We know now that if it's not in use it's not our body. Wisdom dictates that we create a convention for speaking of our body and that we legitimize every instance of expressed dissatisfaction with the human body as a thing, and beyond that as a thing which can be possessed or not.

Does that mean we have no way of describing it when someone loses a finger or a leg? But we have just described it. He has lost a finger or a leg, poor soul. Let's just not go on from there and pretend that his body has been impaired.

Maybe we should borrow from another convention and speak of our body as mystical. It would still leave us with the problem of defining mystical as inclusive of practical, and of practical as conducive to some as yet undefined aim and goal. We would end up comparing

4

'the mystical body' to 'the carnal body' and find ourselves back in a typically modern dilemma, halfway to a solution and comparatively content because left with only half a problem.

The human body is certainly owned and therefore in use. It is the use of it that creates the ownership rather than the other way around. A lot of things we have to own first before we can use them. Legal ownership however does not apply to the human body, which is not a thing. Here use and ownership coincide. It starts with use, because use falls within the scope of possible intention. I can intend to use but not to own.

Use is practical while ownership is powerful. The more things I own, the more powerful I am because of what I can do with them. They afford me more or less power to do or undo, to make or break. So much for the use and ownership of things.

The power that comes along with the ownership of a body is purely and simply the power to do good. The human body is powerful in that it is effective in a good way. But this good way cannot be anticipated in the way that we say we will feed the hungry with more potatoes and that is good or we will prevent or win a war and that is good. The good effect my body or your body has is not of that sort. Of what sort is it then?

In order to answer that question we have to ask: How do we come into the possession and use of the body, which is then practically and powerfully ours? If someone speaks of his body or demonstrates its power by doing good we may well wish to come into the possession of our own. This won't happen unless we recognize

5

the good he does. We will certainly be affected by it but we won't necessarily recognize it. What, for example, if all we recognize is our own inability to do such good? We might just get angry. We might be very angry for having this impotence pointed out to us, coincidentally.

What we then do with that anger is very telling. There is no question as to what we feel like doing. We feel like killing the one who makes us feel so angry. No one likes to be made to feel impotent. Especially if we have some power that is based on our ability to do and undo, to make or break, do we resent having this 'power' cast in the shade and of course ourselves with it, if we identify with it. It is precisely because this pretend power is so much like real power that we cannot bear to be separated from it or to have it undermined. Our human nature craves real power. The extent to which we have become habituated to pretend power is tantamount to the degree of our rage at having it challenged by a power we cannot understand.

Let's call this the rage that brooks no challenge. We cannot afford to let it pass. Our very identity is undermined and we cannot help ourselves, we must do something about it. This is a characteristic of this rage, that we must act on it or act it out. From our present point of view we suppose that it amounts quite simply to our human natural power to do and to act. However we are so to speak otherwise committed. We are hopping on one leg when we might be walking. From within this rage all we can see is that our mobility is being challenged. It's not very complicated once we have overcome the rage somehow and understand what was going on. However at the time, this rage being blind, we 'know' we are right and someone else is wrong. We suppose we know. But this knowledge itself is knowledge after the fact. The fact is that this rage is upon us and we are in its grip. We are possessed by it. No use trying to pretend things are otherwise. Afterwards we like to pretend that 'nothing has happened'. This too is characteristic of this rage. It possesses us for a time, during which we behave and act, and then it leaves us alone and we are once again 'ourselves'. What we feel we have to do now is explain, excuse and justify what we did and how we behaved. As we do so we can feel that rage coming on again. Most of all, therefore, we would like to pretend that it never happened. No one likes to admit that he was out of control, that she spoke hatefully, behaved badly and committed evil actions. Any judge is in a dilemma because the one in the rage is technically not the one after the rage. Not a different person but a different identity is in play.

Nothing could be simpler than telling an individual who is prone to such rages he should accept the responsibility for them. Nothing is harder than telling him how to go about it and actually getting him to do it. What is required, in the end, is the power to do good. The power to do good has to overcome the power to do and undo, to make or break. It might in fact be handy for us if we refer to the latter, supposed power as might. With might you can never tell. It might do or undo. It might make or break. So we might refer to the might of kings, of political leaders and executive directors of corporations. The power the big guy has over the little guy is really might. The one with the gun is mightier than the one without the gun. Might can also be delegated. Then magic and charisma play into it.

Power is always a challenge to might. Those who have no might and are not mighty are least appalled by a show of power and more readily accepting in the face of it. Remember that power, as we use the word here, is good and cannot be bad or do evil.

We also have to realize that might is improbable. This is perhaps a bit more difficult to understand. The probability of a thing implies that we can reflect on it. We cannot reflect on might. Light cannot reflect on itself. It streams out. So from the point of view of the one who is in a mighty rage, there is no way he can come to grips with what is affecting him. He cannot plan a course of action and estimate the consequences. His identity dwindles and he can do nothing about it, nothing, at least, that allows him to continue in his present state of being. Only if he understands what this rage amounts to and what it is about can he take himself to task about it afterwards. What he cannot do is reason himself into a state of acceptance. Reason is mental. The separate mind will not correct the separate body. It will try to suppress it or to set up its supremacy over it, although it can never fully succeed.

The popular mind, as we have seen, is separate from the popular body. Popular reason and popular passion cannot come together. Only as human beings can we behave reasonably and passionately at once. Passion is bodily even as reason is mental. Passion and reason are either disparate or unified. Those who bank on disparate or popular reason will experience passion as an enemy, especially if that passion is also disparate or popular. Equally, those who insist on disparate or popular passion will experience reason as an enemy, especially if reason is also disparate or popular. A civilization that is based on reason subjecting passion is bound to enslave, to view as a potential enemy, a people whose world is shaped in terms of passion objecting to reason. Such is the conflict between black and white. Reason subjecting passion is as immature as passion objecting to reason. It is in their immaturity that these two mutually exclusive points of view may find their common denominator. One type of immaturity will combat another type forever. When individuals step out of their mighty conclaves and become powerful human beings, we are presented with mature being, behaviour and action. Such human beings are naturally, human naturally, capable of both understanding and compassion. They can understand why those who object to reason, especially to popular reason, must not be judged and their compassion for those who subject passion, especially popular passion, to reason allows them to refrain from condemning them.

Passion and compassion are the two fundamental bodily uses. If we are capable of these two, our body is sound. Passion allows us to put up intelligently with injustices to ourselves without insisting on our rights. An insistence on rights is a disembodying exercise. Compassion is what we feel for those who are suffering injustices. Such feeling is an enactment, not a state. Compassion does not happen to us, like happiness or sadness. To feel compassion and to have compassion is the same. If I am suffering an injustice then your compassion will make this easier for me. It will ease my burden.

It seems odd, on first acquaintance, that our fundamental body should come into being in response to injustice. Consider, however, that injustice is always manmade. It arises precisely from a condition of popular thinking or feeling. Precisely where we are not in the possession of our mind or body does a situation of injustice persist. Justice is active (or passive) mind and body as one. Where they are separate, injustice reigns and is readily acted out. And: every injustice, every separation of mental faculties from bodily functions is an opportunity for passion or compassion, in other words for bodily development and growth.

The onus is after all on all of us to turn into human beings and to become more human all the time. We are to own or to possess our body and mind. We are to use them as one. Where we go out on a mental or an emotional limb, this is unjust. If we look for justice, we will find it in a union of thinking and feeling and in an exercise of those faculties which draw equally on the conceptual / cerebral and the visual / passionate aspects of our make-up.

Self-justification is out of the question. It is not a viable option. A useful definition of justice begins with our physical state, when knowledge and understanding truly dovetail. So it's not in circumstances where justice has it roots but in and within ourselves, where certain good habits need to be acquired, sometimes the hard and painful way.

When and while we are unjust we can expect to come up against injustices. If our passion is unruly we are liable to be treated unfairly. This is no excuse for unfair treatment. It is a description of what is liable to happen. If we walk across the street without looking we are liable to be hit by a lorry.

It all begins with ourselves being unjust. Not injust but unjust. In ourselves we have to look for what is liable to happen to us. If our conception is unfounded, then this is an unjustice comparable to our passion being unruly and once again we can expect to come up against injustice. It will seem to us like something we should moan and complain about. What we feel like doing is behaving vengefully. But the injustice is vengeful to begin with. That is what vengeance means.

Vengeance could be called moral gravity. Watch how you go or you fall into a hole. Vengeance is mine, says the Lord. What does that mean, in contemporary terms? It means if you don't care to be human or take steps to become more human, the consequences will be such as to remind you that you neglect something crucial.

Therefore the vengeful god is also the merciful god. Drift away from the love that is gravity and get lost out of orbit. Vengeance keeps you at least in orbit. Understand the real purpose of divine vengeance and get your feet back on the ground. This is eminently desirable.

What we are studying at the moment is our (human) body. We are learning that it has its beginning, like our (human) mind, in our response to perceived injustice.

Irrelevant emotion, like unruly passion, is body in disarray. We don't actually have to wait for an experience of injustice to point this out to us. Of course it depends on our quality of experience and our stage of development. We can notice it in ourselves, when our emotion becomes irrelevant, when our thinking becomes trivial, when our passion becomes unruly or our conception is pointless and unfounded.

When do we become capable of noticing this? When we can compare it to sufficient experience of physical humanity.

For example, once we have a sensible enough notion of universal, personal justice, our unjust, unphysical aberrations will draw themselves to our attention. So we don't have to wait for experiences of injustice to alert us to our perilous state.

Of course we would all like to have some single, simple response at our disposal which would allow us to deal quickly and efficiently with every one of our aberrations as soon as we notice it. Would it do for us simply to assert our physical nature, when it dawns on us that our feeling is once again detrimental? How do you do that? How do you assert your physical nature? How do you reconstitute your whole being when once again you catch yourself being partial, party minded?

The ancient solution is for individual or particular unjustices and piecemeal. It has to be piecemeal because no experience of physical wholeness is available but only its anticipation, as hopefully in the future. Therefore faulty vision, for instance, is counteracted by an adjustment. Here too, in the ancient realm, experiences of injustice, or (divine) vengeance, are not absolutely necessary, but the watchfulness for instances of unjustice is necessarily stressful and laborious. The ancient individual hopes for justice but does not know it in truth, so his response to moments of unjustness in himself can only be piecemeal, i.e. one response to unruly passion, another response to unfounded conception and yet a third to detrimental feeling. However the ancient individual, in spite of this, does not come apart at the seams – because his hope is genuine. It stems from a variety of anticipatory experiences. He repairs his body and rejuvenates his mind when he notices an aberration in himself, although once again, in comparison to a contemporary man or woman, his body and his mind are his own only insofar as he strives to adjust them to the future human being in truth.

So we can shed some light on what it means to be in the possession of one's body by drawing on ancient perceptions for comparative understanding.

A comparison to the modern mind-set is not so simple because modern hope is not genuine. Whole human being is again looked for in the future, but this time history has intervened and whole human being is no longer attainable in future but only here and now.

The modern individual's responses to unjustices he notices in himself are not adjustments, in view of a genuinely hoped for future human wholeness, but justifications, based on what he feels he should be doing but he thinks he cannot, or conditional upon what he thinks might be the case but what he feels might not be the case.

We could almost say that the modern individual is worse off than the ancient, except that, although he does not know it, the physical reality is within his reach and grasp. His salvation depends on him and not on some future event and although he senses this might be so, he supposes it might not.

As we move out and away from the modern dilemma, we have to realize that the contemporary language we develop can no longer express the modern **mind-set** or **body-trend** to the satisfaction of the modern individual and once again, here too, he has to justify himself by insisting on his rights and thereby accentuating his wrongs – so that the contemporary man or woman may deal with him conceptually and compassionately at once.

*

Our body is always in use. If it is not in use, it is not our body. This simple explanation has to be taken on board from the start, lest we suppose that our body is a thing, a tool or an instrument.

Once we have an understanding of our physical or human-natural being and doing, we can come to terms with that aspect of it which is bodily and that which is mental. In this essay I limit myself to an understanding of our body and I mention our mind and its attributes only for the purpose of comparison – and of course so as to remind periodically that our body does not exist separate from our mind.

What use is it to be aware of our body and to know what it is? The answer to that hinges upon the answer to the question: What use is it to be aware of our physical human nature?

The simple answer to the later question must be: The gift of life is not for the unjust and the unrighteous. We would be truly just and righteous so as to have the gift of life. We do not wish to earn this gift, since gifts are not earned. Just and righteous being and doing do not give us the right to the gift of life, for one cannot have a right to a gift. Nonetheless we know that the gift of life is not for the unjust and unrighteous. We also know from experience that we are forever tempted to commit injustice and unrighteousness, thus compromising our readiness and acceptability for the gift of life.

Therefore we welcome insight and ability that allow us to keep ourselves up to the mark. When we know what our body is, (and of course what our mind is) we are in a position to respond creatively to the above mentioned temptation. We will not indulge in self-justification but we will work to further our physical human nature.

And of course this work is to be done in terms of our body and of our mind. As we look within ourselves, and due to the fact that we look within and inward rather than outward, our human nature reveals itself to us, to good purpose, not as a singular entity but in duality, as our body and our mind; as vision and cerebration, as feeling and thinking, and so on, so that for every bodily element there is a fitting, or just, element of mind.

To repeat: Not that our just, physical human nature allows us to grasp the gift of life. It does however place us so close that in good time it will be bestowed. The gift is bestowed where our human nature is just, which is to say: where we own our body and our mind, as one. Where we make the two one, there we will have life.

This is not to say that life cannot be grasped, however that lies outside the province of our present study. When we love our enemy we have life without delay. While we search for the truth we have life within our grasp. When we imbibe the spirit of truth we have eternal life. The righteous man knows that in good time he will have life. At the same time we know that the good time is here and now and if instead of behaving (thinking or feeling) unrighteously we do good, we have life here and now, so that as human beings we are fulfilled. Love of the person next to us is certainly righteous but if that person is our enemy and we love him nevertheless, then we love in a way that puts us in touch with life and in possession of it here and now.

So all the political calculation in the world cannot bring us one step closer to life and while social justice is certainly to be prized it cannot be brought about by political calculation. Let him who seeks social justice begin by looking within himself where the state of his physical human nature, or otherwise, will be revealed to him. Then let him who is full with righteousness be the first to point the accusing finger.

*

We come round now to the practical usefulness of our body. While it's true that we do not own a body that is not in use, and that use and ownership go together, we can still learn a lot by acquainting ourselves with this practicality of our body. If someone were to tell us: "This bicycle is yours while you ride it," we would be able to say a few useful words about what it means to ride a bicycle.

Vision for example. Our senses in use allow us to acquaint ourselves with the world. We have organs of sight, of hearing, of touch, etc. On first acquaintance, the world seems strange and wonderful. We perceive it as in a dream and believe everything. That is childhood in a nutshell. Vision involves believing. Take believing out of vision and you have a shell. A lack of significance. An assurance of your manipulative ego and that's about it. Nonetheless when we look inward we 'see' the seeing and the believing and feel ourselves empowered to go out in the world now with both these faculties intact.

Every time we look inward we discover not only powers for action outwardly but we also come away understanding how these powers can be used, as it were as a left and a right hand. I suppose you would expect that. We might have to go through life for a time using only one hand, showing how we can get on with one hand tied behind our back but happily wisdom intervenes.

So in this case of vision, which is my generic name for all sensing or knowing, knowing and believing show themselves as separable functions. They appear to be distinct and separable. As a child grows up, his vision becomes available to him or her as vision or dream. If he is not brought up, he will stray between the two, one moment all excited by a variety of sensations, and then for a while off inside himself, lost to the world. The upbringing by parental adults is necessary so that he can learn how to dream and know (sense) at the same time.

Even there we have a case, the earliest in life, of 'making the two one'. Heraclitus uses the lovely image of the tensed bow. The two 'horns' come together as the bow is drawn and then action is possible.

So dreaming and knowing, in early life, can separate quite dramatically. One knows of hyper-active, but

17

also of habitually turned-inward children and their conditions can become psychopathic states. Upbringing is necessary from the start for the sake of healthy development. Where such healthy development has fallen behind, or rather where upbringing has been lacking or remiss, education is required. Upbringing is like teaching and education like correction. The sooner we accept these two terms in that way the better.

While it's quite possible to imagine that education may never be required if upbringing is as it should and may be, upbringing, by comparison, is essential and in the absence of it a child disintegrates or becomes extinct. These are rather crass terms, I know but let them stand for the moment. (I use the term 'disintegrate' simply to emphasize the importance of a child's integrity, and 'extinct' to point to the preservation of instinct.)

*

When we speak about the important body-awareness of a child we cannot exclude the parental awareness. Any mature person bringing up, or helping to bring up a child, is aware of that child's body development and understands that inasmuch as it can be identified, it does not exclude parental awareness. So if we point to the duality of vision and dream where a child is concerned we are taking an effective parental presence for granted. A mature man or woman exists in community but a child exists in parental awareness and within this awareness his body can be understood in terms of vision and dream. This duality happens naturally in every young child, so what is needed is whatever will help the child to

18

bring these two together and to unite them in creative activity or passivity.

It becomes evident here that useful body faculties can only be understood in relation to what I have elsewhere called the resurrection principle. In our maturity we readily combine mental and bodily faculties creatively, as one. When we regard our body in distinction we note, similarly, how a duality naturally happens, simply because we are alive, and so that we may function creatively in that way. The resurrection principle means that as we grow to maturity and sustain ourselves in maturity, again and again two functions occur which may be turned into two faculties for the sake of performing one task.

*

As adults we can make a point of knowing and believing at the same time. We can check whether perhaps we are in the bad habit of exercising one of these to the exclusion of the other. If we have done that for a time we will have forgotten that these faculties lie within our jurisdiction. In other words, since we are disembodied to that extent, we will need a stiff reminder and then a period of exercise before our body in that way is in fact ours and intact. How often, for example, do we say: 'I know' when in truth none of our senses are engaged at all and we are not sensible.

If we have for a while been believing without knowing, say, so that even our believing has become defunct, then we can educate ourselves. We can catch up, so to speak, on the knowing, while continuing to do what we previously imagined was truly believing. No doubt the tendency is to run to the other side of the ship so that now it tips down there and once again becomes difficult to keep in line. The educational impulse must therefore also contain the resurrection principle. Our educational exercise must at the same time be creative, which is to say outwardly, not just inwardly, motivated.

Once again let's remind ourselves that the separation of knowing from believing happens, often without our knowing about it for all too long a time. This 'section' is how the resurrection principle first comes into being. It is not something we do but something that is, so to speak, done to us. Let's call it an axiom of human nature, and a rather elementary one for all that. The contradictory nature of every individual, or the very contradictoriness of individuality, points to it as evidence.

Let no one suppose, therefore, that this 'section' can be prevented. It is often misunderstood by those who are trapped in some one-sided notion of progress. They are out on a limb and when they hear the wood creaking and cracking under the strain they climb out even further, 'to avoid the risk' and to 'limit the damage'.

It is unavoidable that as individuals we should be divided in ourselves or die. A worthwhile study would reveal the many ways in which this elementary aspect of the resurrection principle first makes itself felt. A general psychosis sets in, which manifests as particular symptoms. These are frequently admired. They become aims of education, tools of progress, applauded victories of civilization.

Where these primary aspects of non-cooperation with the resurrection principle go unnoticed or even become social motivations, secondary symptoms set in. The madhouses fill because conventional sanity is really a perversion. Individuals are condemned as misfits because they refuse, or are unable, to comply with false strategies and socially sanctioned lies.

Thinking without feeling is as bad as feeling without thinking. Nonetheless we must become aware of both of theses faculties and of the fact that each can be independently pursued. Those who resist their resurrection and fight the section of their indiscriminate and undiscriminating nature need to be shown how to comply in terms of creative exercise. What goes on is certainly fearful but can be explained and shown to be not only unavoidable but also beneficial. Of course only those who are able to be creative, to think and feel at once during creative processes, will find that their approaches to anyone's betterment work and that their arguments for wellbeing carry conviction.

Looking inward to our human nature we find not one single individual entity but two seemingly contradictory potencies. Loosely speaking, there is body and there is mind. There is emotion and there is intellection, there is passion and there is intelligence.

Why do we look inward in the first place? Do we not see all around us organisms perfectly happy strutting their self-assurance, healthy egos in control of the world? It is not until we notice how much of this strutting is an escape mechanisms, how much of the control is aggression, that we begin to wonder.

So why do we look inward? Are we afraid that outside there the solutions may not hold water? Why do we communally turn to one another and away from individualistic ideas and ideologies? Why do we suppose that initially more is to be gained from patient reflection than from adamant self-assertion? Have we heard that the order of reality is within and among us and are we willing, after numerous forays, perhaps, into the realm of popular tradition and convention, to give that a try?

Don't even begin to think that some natures are extravert and some introvert. That would place the emphasis quite wrongly. Certainly some are committed to external preoccupations, to business outside themselves, while others are more preoccupied by what seems to be going on inside themselves. Both however, whether they attempt to see inside or outside themselves, do so with the one cyclopean eye, incapable of perspective.

*

What exactly is the difficulty here? If the resurrection is a cosmic principle, then surely it should come to our attention outwardly as readily as inwardly. The jaundiced eye of the inveterate liar, of the cynic, of the selfish portrayer of the world and of nature, of creation and the universe – of these as some extension of his puerile ego, cannot 'see' anything worth seeing. He or she will rebound from every experience and hear in himself only a distorted echo. He might as well be dead for all the difference it makes to him whether he really lives or dies. Evil urges and drives become evil intentions, then evil behaviour, deeds and actions. Who can say what standard to apply where reality is disconnected from the earth and truth is another word for correct and accurate appearances?

If we contemplate natural creation, we do not look at anything outside ourselves. The only time anything occurs as outside ourselves is when we fail to enlist our own human nature. Practical terms for what this means, to enlist one's own human nature, are well worth looking for. In our second chapter, when we look at how and why we are tempted to make insufficient use of our body, we will have to refer to such terms.

We cannot afford to take the awareness of our human nature for granted. We were born with it, whatever else we were born with. But what does it mean and imply, in addition to that we were born? For a contemporary philosopher at least, the statement: 'I was born' implies birthright and human substance. Recognition of this implication allows him to add that crucial fifth letter of the alphabet to the word 'born'. He knows what it means to be borne. He is carried, as in a stream.

We touch on the genuine luxury of life here. While we know we are born we are borne. We are carried in arms. True and abiding rest cannot be described more significantly.

These are the fundamental prerequirements for being in the possession of our body – and also of our mind, of course. Know what it means to be born. It means birthright and substance.

Birthright means claim to life and knowledge of life. Nothing is more worth having than life or more worth knowing than life. I mean the life that cannot be interrupted by death. If it is interrupted, the resurrection principle kicks in.

These are luxurious insights.

Substance due to birth means both compulsion and desire to live; not to survive, but to live, to live forever. Most of us are rather acquainted with the wish, if not the desire, to live forever and much of our behaviour, along with many of our actions, testify to it. The compulsion to live is more difficult to pinpoint. So often it looks like unfairness, like injustice or evil intention. Because it is compulsive and originates within us we do not readily recognize it until our failure to do so causes it to accost us, from inside or outside ourselves. The more experienced intelligence will identify the compulsion to live more readily where and when it originates within or without us, of necessity unaccompanied by pleasure but happily also still untainted by pain. The contemporary art worker makes it his responsibility to inform and exercise our intelligence in this practical identification of the compulsion to live, both responsibly as it originates unpleasantly within and without us and cheerfully as it wrongly appears to originate painfully inside and outside us.

*

As soon as we enlist our human nature we can see properly. Suddenly our body comes into its own. To see properly means to exercise our body efficiently in that particular way. It also means that our body is right away stimulated in every other way. No one, for example, can be compassionate unless be can see properly. Instead of 'properly' we might say 'human naturally'.

Insight is more fundamental than outlook. There is that notorious difference between seeing and looking in any case; between hearing and listening. Seeing does not depend on being able to look. All the same, those who are able to look and listen do have an advantage. Appearances, after all, are not only 'out there' but also 'out here'.

Cut off from our human nature, we look at and listen to appearances 'out there'. In that way we are adulterous. Our human being is adulterated. Insignificant elements are added and will need to be purged. Some contemporary art is cathartic in that it cleanses our human being, or, more simply, our being, of its insignificant elements.

*

2

Why and how are we tempted to make insufficient use of our body?

Looking and listening to appearances 'out there' is making insufficient use of our bodies. It testifies to a partial separation from our nature. It is one and the same thing, to put it awkwardly.

We are tempted to do so. All our senses, not just seeing and hearing, are open to this temptation if we are not sufficiently enlisting our nature or investing our body. Whatever we sense 'out there', or, for that matter, 'in there', which is to say outside or inside ourselves, is misleading and inoperative. Not truth but falsehood is found in or out there. In the absence of our human nature no truth exists, while falsehood can be said to behave as though it does exist when it fact it does not, except as a mirage or a torn curtain, or a mask.

Falsehood, like all evil, is not only an indication of uninvested body and therefore of unenlisted nature but more crucially of uncreative being and doing or of a lack of creative being and doing.

Creativity, as we know, is 'making the two one'. After the section which results in body and mind, as two distinct and separately accessible and engageable entities or modes of being, we are at liberty to marry the two, creatively. First the section, in perpetuity, then the union, in work. The creative work stands at the end of the resurrection process. The section provides for the wherewithal. But for this distinction, our soul could not enter into the mainstream of reality. Neither, of course, could we.

Not only does our natural being fall apart into body and mind, which are then to exist as 'our' body and 'our' mind, due to our creative behaviour, which in itself only becomes possible on account of this 'falling apart', or section, but equally, as we have observed, does our body then separate and our mind too, so that each is sectioned or cut again, and therefore potentially creative, though of course not on its own.

So our body, upon unavoidable introspection, 'falls apart' into seeing and looking, hearing and listening, feeling and touching and so on.

Even as our massive human natural being, under unavoidable scrutiny, comes apart, leaving us with a body and a mind, so do each of these come apart again, so that we might be creative human beings and whole in ourselves, as contemporary men and women.

I use the word 'massive' here to describe our state, or the state of some part of ourselves, prior to that unkind cut which we do well to anticipate and to welcome. We can anticipate it didactically and welcome it intelligently.

The thing is, we do not automatically avail ourselves of our liberty to be creative. Creativity requires choice and acquires freedom. What we do tend to do, automatically, when our massive nature or some part of it again has come apart, is indulge in partial behaviour. We tend to use the body and not the mind, or we opt for the mind at the expense of the body. Such automatic being and doing precludes our ownership of the body and the mind and true creativity is not possible. All we can come up with are approximations and repetitions of approximations.

These however, inasmuch as they are false or downright evil, do contain an indication of creative possibility. The mistakes we make by acting with one hand tied behind our back are to remind us of the two-handed approach, the possibility of which might otherwise not have occurred to us.

We have the answer here to: Why are we tempted to make insufficient use of our body? The question might also be more accurately stated as: Why are we tempted to invest the body, or body, separately from mind? It is so that we might come around to investing our body creatively in communion with our mind.

The same goes for our human nature. We cannot truly call it 'our' human nature unless and until we enlist it creatively in communion with good spirit, with 'our' good spirit or our god. There is such a thing as massive nature just s there is such a thing as massive spirit. Each testifies to insufficient application on our part. All that is massive is badly experienced, badly perceived and exists as it does only on account of our wickedness. We are always and everywhere liable to be bad and to behave badly. This is what it means to be wicked. We are also mortal, which means we are liable to die. However we do not have to come to a bad or a dead end. We will, however, if we do not strive to possess life.

*

Cosmically, the onus is on creative use of body and mind as one. In that way life is lived. Also action and passion are live.

The same goes for the creative use of nature and spirit as one. That is the greatest teaching. Are you able to discern between massive and human nature? Between massive and good spirit. All that is massive is isolated, neglected, derelict. It cries out in agony for communal existence, for being a member of the family of man.

Not that anything was massive in the beginning. How many people can still remember how it was in the beginning? It seems we need to imagine that. History as data cannot help us. It takes us back, via the ape, to the primordial slime. Not a useful teaching. Creation stories, by comparison, are useful in their own way but then as stories, not as fundamental truths. What we know without believing is just as useless in its way as what we believe without knowing. There is massive believing and massive knowing. They too are temptations. They are ongoing temptations and while we are tempted we suppose we are on the right path and we experience an urgency to continue on that wrong path. It is a broad path and millions trot along it, boosting one another's morale. The narrow path is communal. A few tread it and it leads to the family of man by way of communal existence.

So once again, why is it possible for us to be tempted, to be urged and led into temptation? So that we will espouse the communal solution. In the absence of such temptation, would we not continue only half alive, half human?

To perceive massive culture or civilization, for example, correctly as temptation and therefore to wish to have this evil removed from us, to strain away from it and to seek a good substitute, this is the start in the right direction.

If we perceive that our environment's prevailing cultural stimulations are massive and not communal, we can certainly withdraw from these, not however by isolating ourselves but rather by doing truly creative work, which delivers us from the evil of any indulgence in massive wickedness or mortality. This undoubtedly takes a degree of good willingness and cooperative intention. Massive pursuits, by comparison, take a mere willfulness and intense intention. These produce stupendous marvels which are all useless because contrary to human life and truly communal existence. So much of what is admired as genius, as brilliance, as wonderful, amounts in reality to a massive temptation, no matter how strenuously it parades as culture and civilization, as science or art. Little beginnings with which we cooperate intentionally will bear the fruit of live strength where massive conceptions are bound to collapse under their own weight.

It makes no sense to oppose the massive attempts of those who are tied up or even lost in the temptation of one-sided being and doing because this only hardens them in their resolve. In their minds they are doing right. If their minds or hearts are to be changed it will have to occur to them from within, where they may well be touched, moved and even eventually motivated, however due to examples of creative communality that are freely set, in their presence, so to speak, and in no way contentiously.

Those who are happy and content in massive being and doing are furthest away from true happiness and contentment and only examples of blessedness might shake them in their misguided resolve.

*

A more specific answer to the question: How are we tempted? might be: impatiently, enviously and greedily.

We make insufficient use of our body inasmuch as we flee from – well, let's call it, in a nutshell and sum totally: from the wrath of God. This is a complicated issue. What we have in mind as God is massive spirit, not good spirit. Without doubt this amounts to a threat. We run away from it – speedily. Our preoccupation with speed is at times wonderful to behold. What we neglect to do is to blame this wrathful and jealous 'God' on ourselves. While we run away from Him He pursues us. Were we to stand still and to listen patiently to his message, then this god would produce in us a splendid change of heart, of which we would have more reason to be proud than of our great variety of speed records.

Patience, however, is a communal pursuit. In order to be truly patient I must apply my body and my mind in unison. That is unique. To be patient and to do patiently is not a massive but a communal art. The 'wrath of God' cannot touch us. Meanwhile the love of god, the love that is god, operates on our behalf. Is that not well worth knowing?

*

So we are tempted impatiently to neglect 'our' body, even to lose it, and to charge away into the impersonal blue on our mere mentality, where everything is minimal-mathematical. But then it was not, after all, our own body we neglected. It was massive body we had not yet invested. What it finally comes down to, when all the pertinent facts are considered and when we insist on saying only what we can say clearly, is that we neglected to be creative and communal. Both body and mind were available to us, due to that unavoidable resurrectional section, and instead of behaving creatively and 'making the two one' as we act, we slipped off into mere, massive body, in some way. We must have, otherwise that impatient reaction, that temptation would not have set in. I think we should understand this quite thoroughly. We should try to understand it not so that we can prevent ourselves from sliding into such one-sided, bodily indulgences in future but so that we will recognize the temptation of the resulting impatience for what it's worth. It is worth something. We learned that when we asked why

31

we were tempted. It is to coax us in the direction of proper physical, creative communality.

Prior to that resurrectional section which made body and mind accessible for us as separate entities we really had no way of knowing how arbitrary and egotistical our being and behaviour was. The ancient expression 'sinning' applies here. Not the modern, but the ancient meaning of 'sin' applies. Prior to that unkindly cut we didn't know we were sinning. Now we know. We can tell because of this tempting impatience.

Well, I am unsure now, is it really the ancient meaning of sin I mean? Was the ancient meaning – or rather is the ancient meaning – not tied up with observance of rules and regulations? The ancient meaning of 'body and soul' is after all so different from the modern, and then even more from the contemporary, meaning.

This takes us too far outside our present study. Enough said that the contemporary meaning of sin, if we wanted to resurrect that term, would have to refer to that murky area of action and experience where we do not respond appropriately to our divided self (body and mind) but we linger in, or indulge ourselves in, one or the other of those two halves of our self.

The contemporary philosopher looks at that famous advice, that we pray: 'Lead us not into temptation but deliver us from evil' and understands it in the following way: I really and truly do not want to get caught up in impatience, in envy and greed, and prefer instead to be and to behave creatively and communally. Then he examines carefully, in that good spirit of creative communality, how these temptations arise, especially in himself and how they can be explored and exploited as soon as possible, practically, once they come into being. After all he wants to show how that crucial step can be taken in ourselves from the recognized impatience, envy and greed and the like, to the good doing.

Greed, therefore, is not a sin but a sign of sinfulness, if we want to be perfectly consequent and not just abstract-theological. It's no good trying to get rid of envy or impatience by suppressing it, by trying to be no longer, or not again, greedy, envious or impatient. That does not work. It's wrong-headed. It's ill-informed. It testifies to an outdated, modern, notion of what wickedness is. Modern man tries to be good by suppressing his wickedness. What bunkum! How absurd on two counts: We cannot be good and wickedness cannot be got rid of by suppressing it.

However we are not here to make modern man feel bad. What good would it do to make him feel bad about himself? He feels bad enough already. Hence the impatience, the envy and the greed. Besides are there not in ourselves still many pockets of modernity? How often are our reactions not modern! Impatiently we criticize and condemn and then we hate ourselves for 'not having been good'.

Of those who are perfectly happy being impatient, envious and greedy we cannot really speak here. They are surely in a category of their own. They revolt us and on reflection our hearts go out to them but alas! Let him who is not wicked cast the first stone. Let him who is not mortal be the first to criticize the dead.

*

The one who lives and creates is not tested or tempted. It is the one who makes inappropriate use of nature or spirit, of body or mind, of knowledge out there or of knowledge in there. It makes sense that he should be reminded of his one-sided approach to life and the world. Not only does it make sense but it makes merciful sense. Along with the reminder, the painful and inconvenient reminder, always comes the hint on how to repair the self-caused damage. We need only to put up gladly with the inconvenience and to suffer the pain intelligently for the creative tool to be handed to us.

The same test or temptation of impatience which seems to urge us to indulge in mere massive body or in mere massive mind also works to remind us of one-sided body indulgence, where we merely know, without believing, or we try merely to believe, without knowingly. More damage has been done in Christendom, for example, by equating faith with mere, massive believing, separate from knowing.

It is not that knowing and believing are separately accessible, or that vision and dream are separately perceivable but that we do not unify them, that is the true cause of impatience. Of course we can do the wrong thing and the bad thing in that one-sided way, which gets us deeper into trouble, but it's not any use just to stop doing those wrong and bad things. We cannot do it for long anyway. Only when we begin to do the right and the good thing are we out of danger. That should be a simple enough lesson to learn, but how often do we not suppose we help others and improve them by pointing out to them what they are doing badly and wrongly? Not criticism, but the example of right and good doing helps and heals.

*

Vision and dream need to be creatively conjoined in our work. That goes for knowing and believing too. But what about feeling? We say we feel 'like' – going for a walk or throwing up. We know how much somebody can get concerned with how they feel and they get so engrossed in their 'feelings' that we cannot help wondering if selfishness has them in its grip. We know how to differentiate between feeling, which is something we do, and a feeling, or feelings, which come over us and are not voluntary or intentional. So we need to ask: When feelings beset us, pleasant or unpleasant, what will we do so that our feeling is intentional again? Is it simply a matter of willing or intending, or is some other faculty involved? Certainly it makes no sense to suppress our feelings because they merely reappear as emotions. And if we repress our emotions we will eventually fly into a passion. We all know how readily we get hurt if for a while we have indulged our feelings or emotions and then, so as not to get hurt so soon again, we repress them. Then we have to kill off our passions, after we have been carried away by one, to our detriment.

Feeling, emotion and passion, along with sensation, make up the sum total of our body, which is creatively in use. That much is clear. What is not so clear at this stage is how emotion and passion can be intentional, as they must be if we are to think of them as part of our body in use.

35

If we substitute suffering for passion, we may be halfway to an answer. However we must take care not to confuse suffering with pain. Pain is a passion. When we are in pain we are not necessarily suffering. Suffering is in fact intentional and voluntary. It's what we do when we stop resisting a pain and instead we trust it to inform and to intuit us. I use 'intuit' in the sense of in-teaching.

So there at least we have a productive way of dealing with our passions. As in the case of all the other body-parts, the only way we can stop resisting, suppressing or repressing, is by conjoining the left with the right in creative unison.

What I am trying to do at the moment is to identify the massive left and the massive right. I recognize the danger of wanting to be entirely schematic in my approach. Modern conventional usage of language does however reflect many centuries of one-sided activity and passivity. One feels one is slashing one's way through a thorny hedge or through a jungle of clinging creepers. Surely this testifies to my own immaturity in this particular realm of endeavour. I guard above all against impatience.

I know that my entire body depends on my vision being clear. Clarity of vision is crucial. When I have a vision I pay no attention to it, on purpose. It might move me impressively but I take nothing from it; I treat it like an accident which is to lead me mercifully towards improved vision.

A new element has appeared here. Instead of improved vision I could also say increased vision. Clarity is one thing, growth and increase is another. Our faculties are not only to be distinct and useful but they are also to get stronger. Never underestimate the effect an increase of strength can have on our make-up. It could be that by pursuing this element of growth and increase, we will arrive at a few solutions to some of the problems that have arisen during my attempt to observe the effects of the resurrection principle on massive bodily phenomena.

Strength succeeds resurrection. This we can take for granted. All our faculties are equally to partake of this strength. That is to say, all our creative faculties are to partake – and to grow stronger. How then are those bodily parts affected which are still massive and not taken up into any creative process?

Their massiveness is highlighted. This we experience as languor and lassitude. An ill-defined heaviness sets in. This goes on at the same time as our productive and creative faculties are strengthened. We must have some, by the way, or there would be no influx of strength. Mind you, no particular faculties are pinpointed necessarily by this languor and lassitude. It affects us indiscriminately. It is up to us, first of all, to know what is going on and to understand why it is going on.

Then of course we will wish to know what we can do, if anything, to take advantage of this merciful affection. We don't just want to put up with it. We believe we are affected for a perfectly good reason. This is where our earlier discovery of intuition comes into its own. We may in perfect good faith believe that while this languor and lassitude is upon us, we are being taught. All that matters is that we rise to the occasions of being taught. What counts is that we stay around and don't absent ourselves. It is of the essence that we *abide*. While we wait and hold out we are taught. New faculties are established. Patience, here too, is of the essence. The very faculty which we are to gain must be tested. We incur the temptation of impatience, envy or greed. Of course we would wish to be able to sidestep these. Indeed it may be possible to the extent that we keep in mind that we do after all wish to be rid of as much of our massive self as possible and that indeed we desire to be stronger. Within such a framework of ambition and insight we will be tempted no more. Impatience is replaced by patience, envy by contentment and greed by satisfaction.

*

So with the onset of new strength, what needs to go on is that we rise to the occasion and then our present faculties are fortified or increased and new ones are established.

'Rising to the occasion' is an intuitive exercise. We practice the willingness to be 'intuited', as we are intuitive. The slightest feeling of weakness can be our signal. Now it is time to be intuitive again.

However we can also do intuitive work. Some are especially gifted to do this. They are rightly called teachers. They know that strength succeeds resurrection and they live this truth. They are willing to partake of the weakness of others and to exemplify it as strength. How they go about doing this must be entirely up to them, so obviously such a true teacher could not sell his services, such as in a public or private school system. He depends on free, interpersonal relationship. In our western culture this gift is mostly processed in writing. Literary tuition, or didactic writing, is in a category of its own.

*

Let's see now if we can make any headway in terms of our previous pursuit of bodily phenomena as unifiable dualities.

Wherever we wrongly supposed we were in the possession of a body, in other words, where we mistakenly referred to our body when in truth we had none but were more or less in bondage, susceptible on this side to every elementary fluctuation and addicting ourselves on that side to one false image after the other, there, on either side, we should now be able to identify potential faculties, which are accessible separately but useless except in conjunction with their counterpart. While they must each be accessible for creative use, they are at the same time temptations into which we may fall or stray. Let us assume that we have attested to our willingness to be intuitively alert at all times, or at least as often and as much as we can every day, so that we will not need to be tempted. We do however know how to behave if we do fall or stray into temptation, so there is no need to panic. Nonetheless there is every reason to be intuitively awake and alert. Do we not after all espouse the resurrection principle precisely so that the coming strength and life will be ours? It is ours now, while we work within sight of the end of our human existence, which is eternal life here and now.

So what exactly do we intend to identify here? Surely no palpable difference exists between any temptation and that which tempts. We are not concerned with moral standards here but we desire to recognize ethical processes, so that we may behave ethically, which is most useful for us as fulfilled human beings.

I believe therefore it would make most sense if we identified *moods* on one side of the section and *distempers* on the other.

A discussion of this would now bring to its conclusion the chapter on why and how we are tempted to make insufficient use of our body.

Both good moods and bad moods are massive and therefore tempting. Good moods promise indulgence while bad moods foster resistance. More accurately, pleasant moods promise more and greater indulgence while unpleasant moods foster more and greater resistance.

It is therefore quite possible to identify all moods by what they promise or foster. Impatience, envy and greed all play their role.

With distempers the story is not much different, except that here we are in the grip, right from the start, of chaotic feelings, emotions and/or passions. All feelings, emotions and passions are of course chaotic but when they surprise us we have a problem on our hands. What we tend to do is react. We start an argument or a war. We make enemies of others and a nuisance of ourselves. We lay blame and stir up acrimony. And all the time we presume we are in the right. If anyone tries to correct us we flare up into violence.

The resurrecting section leaves us with those two massive, bodily complexes of phenomena if we pay no attention. Resurrection may be viewed as an event, as a series of events or as cosmic influence in our existence. However we view it, the bodily results are distemper and moodiness. (We disregard vision and all the senses for the time being and limit ourselves to feeling, emotion and passion.)

Both distemper and moodiness are affected by impatience, envy and greed. We are always susceptible to these three. None of us are good. All are liable to badness and wrong-doing. In that way all are wicked. Those who distinguish between the good and the wicked are talking nonsense, however eloquently they are defended as guardians of tradition. A contemporary philosopher can speak with true authority because nothing removes him from the everyday life of his generation. He is a 'priest after the order of Melchisedek'. What we need to look at now is how moodiness and distemper can be reversed. Feelings, emotions and passions are involved in both cases. What I mean by that is: With every mood we are in, and in every case of distemper, along come envious feelings, impatient emotions, greedy passions, or any mixture of these. How could anyone unravel it all? Emotions can be envious, feelings impatient, passions might be all three. The only reason we can make even that much discriminate sense of it is that we have to that minor extent assented to the resurrection principle rather than rejecting it out of hand. We have taken advantage of at least some of the strength available.

The identification, even on this lowest level, is crucial if we want to get ahead. With every consignment of new strength come further tests and temptations, for which we can be ready or which may bowl us over. So we have to ask ourselves: Do we want to make progress or not? Let's face it, this is the only progress really worth making, because it lasts. We can buckle down to it, we can learn and practice at our own pace and no one or nothing can disabuse us of our conquests.

What we have identified as moods and distempers, then, might be described as the two disjointed sides of the same false coin. What we would like to bring about, in the interest of ethical work and of our personal growth, is the genuine coin, with face and obverse qualities. Not fake or adverse, but face and obverse.

Clearly, from a sensible point of view, we may take responsibility for that part of our body which we might describe as heart-centred, or heart-related. Vision and all the senses pertain to our head, whereas feeling, emotion and passion pertain to our heart. They all come together in our creative work as embodiment.

Moods and distempers we may take note of individually. Often we flip from a mood to a distemper and back again. Ego is involved. Selfishness plays a role. We don't want to be torn this way and that by discordant body components. That shuts us up inside ourselves rather than allowing us to flourish communally.

Bad moods and good moods should be readily identifiable because they do us the disservice of stifling our creativity. We find it difficult to love because either we are wrapped up in the pleasures of the self, full of ourselves, or we are down-hearted, discouraged, despondent. You might ask yourself: Am I in a mood? Is that what is holding me back and hanging me up? Am I once again full of that kind of enthusiasm and high spirits that usually ends in a 'downer'; in pessimism and hopelessness?

In short, we can learn to distinguish between moods and mood.

Not that we want to spend time analyzing our good or bad moods. That is morbid and leads nowhere. We just want to notice them, so that we can counteract them. Even reading what I have written here will help because it does help me.

The transformation from moods to mood depends on our merciful recognition of the former. How is it merciful? In that I am perfectly aware of my natural wickedness, which is to say: of my inborn liability to be bad and do badly, and at the same time also of my ability to do good, to be ethical and truly powerful.

This merciful approach to myself and to others is crucial. The opposite, and totally wrong-headed approach would be the judgmental one. Here we suppose that we, and others of course, can be good and as a consequence we are never done criticizing and being contemptible. I know whereof I speak because this is one of my greatest failings. I am ever so aware of the damage one can do by forgetting one's own wickedness and mortality. So mercy is really and truly of the essence. There is more to it than just accepting that we are bound to make mistakes. The will to live and to be live overrides all that. We have to dig a little deeper in ourselves if we wish to be creatively effective. Besides, we are not bound to make mistakes at all. That just isn't true. We are not bound at all and that precisely is often the problem, when we seek a negative certainty, at least a negative certitude, in a kind of fateful necessity about ourselves. No, we are totally and entirely at liberty, by definition and in fact. Circumstances cannot play into that. Slaves and prisoners sometimes demonstrate this, much to the consternation of the poor souls who enslave and imprison them for no other reason than that they think of them as bad and of themselves as good. The captor has behaved mercilessly while the captive is still at liberty to be merciful. We have a fine literary example of this in Laurens Van der Post's story: 'The Seed and the Sower'. Elsewhere, if I recall correctly, he speaks of an "inward-bound school which imprisonment under the Japanese had been".

Merciful recognition of distempers has an effect similar to the one due to such recognition of moods. We begin by feeling aggravated, uncertain and driven and then, upon merciful recognition of this, temperance sets in and we are tempered. Mood and temperament together then make for true character.

A murderous temper can flash up and flare out in no time, we know this all too well. Similarly a rotten mood can fester suicidally, in silence. Once our new body has begun to develop, this is the area we have to attend to. Here the most dire emergencies arise, all too frequently with tragic consequences.

*

Moods and distempers do not coincide. We are either moody (in *a* mood) or distempered (in *a* temper). On that massive level we are not in possession of our body but rather reminded of that fact by, so to speak, half a body. Or, if we can remember that our body is head and heart, i.e. sense and compassion (vision – sight, hearing, touch, taste, smell and feeling, emotion, passion) we can say that on the massive level we are not in possession of the lower half of our body, the heart half, and what's more, only half of that again, moodiness or distemper, is forcing itself to our attention.

This is turning into quite a tour of discovery. Not only are we learning to distinguish between owned body and tempting body but we are also gaining fresh insight into the very make-up of our body. It may be quite useful, as a result, to distinguish between head and heart as the upper and lower half of *our* body. These would be more like spheres of reference for learning purposes and certainly not separate parts. Moods and distempers are disparate; they do not coincide in an individual or person.

Your lower body, your heart, is compassionate. This means that you are in possession of your feeling, emotion and passion. When this falls apart into feelings, emotions *or* passions you no longer (or not yet) own them. It might be useful to refer to them then collectively as 'the passions', as long as we keep in mind that this is a collective term. It would allow us to refer to massive body as senses (sights, sounds, tastes, etc.) and passions (feelings, emotions, passions), while sense (common sense?) and compassion would refer to our entire, owned body, in creative use. Among those who are in the possession of their body, some have more common sense and others more compassion but all must have both. The two are not opposites, striving in different directions, nor are they isolated, non-coincidental extremes but more like a team of two horses.

Our entire body can also be compared to a team of four, the vision and sense of the upper, head half and the passion and compassion of the lower, heart half.

Behold, the resurrected body reminiscent of the crucified body!

*

Before we deal with the question: How does our body compare to our flesh, let's have a closer look at what I have called the resurrection principle.

This makes sense as soon as we posit the end or goal of existence as life. Not until then does everything fall into place, including our ownership of body and flesh (and mind, of course).

In other words, resurrection must be what we are and not just something we think about. It is what we are, within ourselves and a kind of heightened awareness will allow us to come to terms with it. This does away once and for all with such a thing as inward states, which always get in the way of clear thinking and true feeling. It also obviates excesses and shortcomings in our behaviour, both mental and bodily, because we do not advance until we are ready and we do not lag behind when we should be ready.

Naturally we wish to be resurrected. This goes without saying, although a thousand actions and activities testify to this wish under a different label or name. Conven-

tionally the word 'resurrection' is used to describe transformation from dead to living. No wonder, then, that we
need to know life as eternal. To be born again implies being borne differently. You leave the country of your birth,
where catastrophe reigned and arrive in a different country, where suddenly everything seems possible, but you
have to learn the language, and this takes time. But let's
not get bogged down in resurrection tropes. The talisman
of a materialist society, for example, is the future god who
makes everyone who is anyone happy. He dares you to
believe, therefore, that your society, the society you live
in, would for that reason prefer it if you were happy now.
If you cannot manage this, either kill yourself or buy into
the materialist resurrection.

'The' resurrection is of course mythic. If anyone
says: "I am the resurrection" he means that through him
or her that particular mythic reality becomes concrete and
corporeal. For us what matters is that we are continually
resurrected. This is possible only if we continue to resurrect. To the extent that we help others from forms of
death to forms of life, we ourselves live.

For us, 'the' resurrection no longer needs to be
mythic but it can be historic, which is good news because the arduous, ground-breaking task has been done
for us. Also, since it has been done, it cannot be done
again. Sadly many people's pride is hurt by this. I look
at it practically. I take advantage of what has been
made available and as a direct consequence I can do
even greater things than the one who made it available.
That is hard to swallow by traditionalists who would
rather gather at the feet of their hero in adoration than

tread the path he pointed out and do the work he made possible. Your fundamentalist traditionalist even has to defend his adored hero against anything but adoration, thus becoming his enemy in reality.

Historic resurrection has to be learned and then it operates in and as our human nature. This 'in and as' is rather important. Prior to learning resurrection we are apt to view our human nature as either human or natural. I know this sounds a little convoluted but consider how the humanist and the naturalist live in different camps. The humanist proposes a peculiar and exclusive emphasis on effective personalities and tribal elements, while the naturalist devotes himself insistently to series of cause-and-effect-linked forces, mechanisms and laws. It's easy to see how the two, the humanist and the naturalist, face away from each other. Perhaps without realizing it, they nowhere tread on common ground. They find themselves in the pursuit of myths, in the above mentioned way. Or rather not they themselves but those who embrace human-natural resurrection find them there. Once being found, there is no reason why they should not face each other. But that is another story.

Once historic resurrection has been learned, we have said, it operates in and as our human nature: *in* it inasmuch as we live and breathe it and *as* it insofar as we direct our actions, deeds and behaviour. Our constitution and our organization dovetail, both transitively and intransitively.

*

3

How does our body compare to our flesh?

Flesh, not specifically yours or mine now, we can always point to and we can point it out to one another. We say: This is one thing, and: That is another, and what we mean is carnal characteristics which identify something for us. "That is an orchid," you say, "a lady's slipper," and what you point to is broad, lanceolate, ribbed, pale green leaves, a solitary flower with maroon-coloured sepals and a large yellow lip, and so on. Those are some carnal characteristics of Cypripedium calceolus, which help to identify this rare and beautiful flower. The carnal characteristics are innumerable. We decide for ourselves when to stop looking for more.

The names we give to things, then, allow us to refer to them as carnal beings, to the extent that they are carnal.

As human beings we are not only spiritual but also carnal. We would like to distinguish, however, between carnality that is accidental and carnality that is owned. If I am at peace and at home with myself as a creature of flesh and blood I can truly say that my flesh is my own. It means not only that I am able to put up with what cannot be changed but much more that I understand the perfectly good reason for being such a creature and am therefore strongly in favour of it. It also means that my mortality and my wickedness are no longer fundamentally problematic for me. I understand them as liabilities and connect them in my mind with privileges.

My flesh, therefore, is what I mean when the carnality of this creature which I am is taken up into the resurrection process which operates on my behalf and with which I co-operate. I cannot really and truly refer to it as *my* flesh if I think of it as: a. – a hindrance to my spiritual development, or b. – the be all and end all of my existence on earth. Neither the sensualist nor the spiritualist can be said to be in possession of 'his' carnal being or nature. We would only call it theirs because it pertains to them, which is quite different from ownership, which implies responsibility.

So as soon as we take creative responsibility for carnal characteristics which help to define us, we can be said, to that degree, to possess our flesh – rather than ourselves being possessed by it.

*

But what does this mean, that carnality is 'taken up into the resurrection process'?

From the point of view of carnality this sounds absurd. But then let's face it, from that point of view our new body sounds absurd, so there's no need to worry about that. It's enough if from our own point of view we understand and are in no doubt about the suitability of our carnal being to our spiritual being.

Our new and spiritual body can on that account be described as incarnate. This should not be seen as of any advantage to our corporeality. However our carnality is now no longer a drawback or a liability in the sense that we are bound to be creatures of the flesh and susceptible to its environmental vagaries.

Again, now it finally makes sense to speak of 'our ' flesh. But how exactly is it taken up into the spiritual growth process, which we call the resurrection principle?

What we need is a suitable image of 'our' flesh, so that this can become clear. We are by no means the first to search for such an image. Wherever anyone feels spiritually inclined, even 'called' if not 'chosen', his carnality becomes problematic, and this precisely because he is bound to sense that his flesh is after all *not* his; at least not as he has been in the carnal habit of knowing it. He has thought of it as his while in the bloom of healthy youth, but with adulthood and its tests and temptations have also come the challenges to this view of his carnal self being in his possession, in the sense of 'under his control', and so he has had to make adjustment to his view on account of sickness, illness and death. Youth luxuriates under the illusion of immortality and this illusion has to be faced as such with the advent of adulthood. It has to be faced if it is not voluntarily faced. The adjustments he feels called upon to make testify to the problematic state of his carnal being. He tries to cope by using imagination. He is grateful for having the use of this faculty, for being able to bridge the gap between his view of his carnality, as his, and his experience of it, as a law onto itself. He strives eagerly to get behind this law and to trace it to its source but the best he can do, as we know from historic evidence of different cultures world-wide, is come up with a great number and variety of laws, all of which are imagined in one way or another. When a creative poet uses an image, he solves, or even dissolves, for the time being, the problematic state due to our carnality viewed as 'ours' while experienced decidedly as not ours. Exu-

51

berant joy, grave despair, anxiety, boredom, terror – all draw to our attention the need for a point of view from which we may recognize our carnal being as truly ours.

It's almost as if the correct point of view were enough. Of course it isn't. However, the nature of the case is such that as soon as we have the correct point of view we also have the reality – and vice versa. So we have the choice of attacking the problem from the left or from the right. We may look to our point of view, our spiritual understanding, or instead we may go by our experience and discover the truth of it. In either case what we will come up with is our flesh, or carnal being, as truly ours and no longer in contradisposition to our creative being and growth.

Take experience first. Common sense and compassion, as we have learned, are not empty words but functions of our willingness to be human, to be spiritually alive and ethically active. Now if we ask ourselves: How do we know we are being compassionate and what makes us think we are being commonsensical, in the profound sense of the word? we might answer: We just know. This 'just knowing' seems to be of significance, as if we were justified in our original being and doing. After all, it's not as if we had to convince someone else. Our business is compassion and common sense and making sure that we are and continue to be, under circumstances as they come about, compassionate and commonsensical. It is not our business to persuade others that we are genuine but to be genuine. So what matters is that we really and actually mind our business. If we come into conflict with those who plead with us or even insist that we justify ourselves, we will simply continue to mind our business.

And here, especially thus confronted and in the face of such challenges, we realize that our body is incarnate. We can bring our mind into play and think it through, eliminating all that is false, wrong or just plain inappropriate to the case in hand, or we can simply know the justice of our flesh as it makes our genuine human being and doing knowable for us.

The experience we mean, therefore, is ethical existence carnally manifested. It is the experience of ourselves as creative creatures which is made possible by just flesh – for which we may be grateful, by the way. 'Just flesh' is the image we were looking for and it serves our purpose marvellously.

This just flesh is ours. We possess it. This does not mean that we can make use of it in some way. It is not a faculty, or a function of our soul, like our body and mind. So in that sense it differs from our body. It just is. However it is like our body, and not different from it, in that we own it, which implies that it will not turn against us, surprise us with sudden vagaries or leave us in the lurch.

An additional attribute may be mentioned. If we are grateful for it, as indeed why not, it is nourishment. It is sustenance. If we wonder why gratitude should be essential we only have to consider that it is not through our own efforts that we have come into possession of it. All we have done is realize that *this is so*.

In the prayer Christians refer to as the Lord's prayer this sustenance is mentioned initially as *epiousios*, in mistranslation as 'daily bread', and indeed its importance for our existence in the light of day cannot be overestimated. Since we no longer need to ask for this as a gift in the future however (aorist imperative of 'give') since we have it here and now, it remains for us to be grateful for it, so that nowadays Christians might pray: "Thank you for our daily bread, our true sustenance", by which they would mean, in terms of experience, this just knowledge, this realization of their bodies as being incarnate and of their flesh being in fact their flesh.

*

Looking to our point of view, to our spiritual understanding, as we said we would, and fully expecting to come to the same conclusion as when we checked on our experience – of incarnate body or of flesh taken up into the resurrection process, we find that we have to begin by opening ourselves to merciful spirit, which contains within itself an incalculable element, an element which no human can fathom. Always and again we come up against that which reveals in us the brute if we pit ourselves against it and blesses our true human nature as soon as we submit to it. Only on a very trifling and superficial level must it seem contradictory to us that the 'one' who would nurture and nourish us is also the one who punishes. Meanwhile wisdom shows with clarity that rebellion against mercy is in fact, in itself, punishment. There is no interval of deliberation on the part of a judge. Resistance against wisdom is one thing. Wisdom interprets the means and weighs or apportions consequences. Mercy operates outside time. As soon as we resist merciful spirit, and by dint of doing so, we undergo correction and suffer improvement – unless, of course, we continue to resist, in which case we become increasingly less able to comprehend the truth of the situation.

Learning mercy is therefore one of our most formidable tasks and certainly the one that comes least naturally to us. In no way, however, does that mean that as human beings we are naturally rebellious. Only an inherently judgmental attitude would lead to such a conclusion. No, what has to be taken on board here is that human naturally we are neither merciful nor rebellious. It is not until spirit of mercy applies itself to us that we are bound, then, initially, to close ourselves to that which is, after all, in that sense alien to us. Therefore, to put it metaphorically, merciful spirit could not possibly hold it against us that we are not, initially, able, so to speak, to digest it.

By the same token it must be obvious then that since we are not by nature rebellious, and since this rebelliousness is to all intents and purposes brought about by merciful spirit, we are equally bound to experience our rebelliousness as alien to us, as unnatural to us and suddenly we are trapped in a typically modern and tragic situation. Merciful spirit will not go away. We have only the one choice: to learn mercy or to commit suicide. An insistence on resistance, after all, is suicide. We do not resist a passing comfort or convenience after all, but that which sustains us, which is very life for us.

The question has to be asked: If that is the way of it, on what basis can anyone choose 'very life'? I suppose if someone were to show me how to do it I might imitate and follow. What about him, though? How was he able to learn mercy, if no one is born with it, with neither the ability for being merciful nor with the capacity for recognizing merciful spirit?

It's an insoluble problem. Wisdom is not able to solve it. Mythological trickery always comes in handy but then there are always a few who refuse to demean themselves and because of them, because of their resistance until it is broken, merciful spirit gains a precious foothold in human nature. That very aspect of our human nature which rebels is also the respect which allows merciful spirit to take human nature in stride.

However even this 'being broken' by merciful spirit is a very specific phenomenon. Only a very peculiar type of resistance, which must be honest, authentic and genuine, can result in merciful spirit being ingested or imbibed. Keep in mind that rebellion may be ideological and political, psychic, materialistic etc. It may be cowardly, false, corrupt. It is only authentic rebellion against merciful spirit which can result in human natural mercy – which may then be described as acquired or received. Leniency, clemency, magnanimity – these are all possible purely from our original human nature, but mercy must be learned. Doesn't it make us wonder who was the first to learn it?

If we knew that, we could learn mercy from him. That would save us a lot of painful revolt. Or we could learn it from anyone who has learnt it from him.

*

So we must assume that the first human natural being to learn mercy must have resisted honestly, authentically and in a genuine way. There is no doubt that at first he must have resisted and rebelled. The fact that he was able to resist with his entire being would have made the difference. That was what made him unique at the time, that he resisted merciful spirit not politically, or psychically, or ideologically but with his whole natural self, including his carnal self.

No one can say that until then no one else might have performed the feat. The point is, that no one else did and that he did. Why did he come up with sufficient honesty, authenticity and genuineness? *He just did.*

If we are – or rather *since* we are – also carnal, and if our whole being is also carnal, as we know it is, then when we resist merciful spirit with our whole being, we do so also carnally. We do not resist merely carnally, which would be a case of living by the sword and also then of course, when this is broken, of dying by the sword, and we do not resist with all of our being except our carnality, which would be a way of living mythologically, and then dying mythologically, so that our carnal self during living and dying falls away. Both the mythological and the militant way of living and dying usually get highly organized and this is a defensive move against merciful spirit. It too must eventually be broken. What is revealed then, unavoidably, is that the resistance to merciful spirit was not whole and death ends up being organized too, which leaves us in the realm of apocalypse.

It would be silly to suggest that we, or anyone else for that matter, know fine well when we resist merciful spirit that we do so. All we know is that we are up against something which seems to constrain us. It interrupts what we know as our natural development and we must face up to it if we are not to become inauthentic. It constrains us both inwardly and outwardly. Outside and inside constraints, by comparison, are merely to make it obvious that what we have to face, if we want to live and not die, also suits our carnality and does not exclude it. The outside constraint is to make it obvious to us that the merely carnal, or militant, resistance is in vain just as the inside constraint shows us that the carnal aspect of our nature is not to be excluded in the merciful transformation. So if our affairs don't go right, we are being merely carnal and if we are unhappy or sick it is time to bring our carnality more thoroughly into the equation. In both cases we do well simply to dismiss the failure and to turn away from it, as we turn towards merciful spirit, by *just knowing* and *just doing*.

*

It's important that we know the difference between our body and our flesh, and that we know how the one compares to the other. We get into difficulties when we mistake one for the other. Knowledge of merciful spirit is paramount. That is what keeps our body alive, so that it may be live. But what of our carnal being? We are flesh and blood too. It is our knowledge of merciful spirit that informs us of that spirit's incarnate tendency. Mythologically we might say that merciful spirit wishes or desires to be incarnate. As we were born, 'our' flesh is not our own truly. As we grow and develop, merciful spirit infuses us. Let us not call it influence now but infusion. We grow to maturity. In our youth we suppose we are all in one. We have a foretaste of ripeness. We may know merciful spirit by proxy. In our youth we may be foolish and mistake the foretaste for the reality. To that extent then we will be disillusioned. Therefore let youth be the time of learning. Not only of training but of learning.

It is merciful spirit which infuses our whole being, including our flesh and blood. Therefore let us not only know, but also learn. Define learning as an extension of knowledge into the realm of the flesh. If we learn but know not we end up with straw. If we know but learn not we have a great deal but come up against difficulties and diverse troubles.

Conventionally these words are not used like that. We have to be willing to step outside convention. Knowing is not the same as learning. Merciful spirit, as we know, infuses our common sense and we welcome it. Knowledge, then, is the commonsensical reception of merciful spirit. But merciful spirit goes on from there. Feelings, emotions, passions are all carnal. Hatred, envy, greed are carnal. Merciful spirit infuses our heart too. Our heart is the seat of these. How shall they be dislodged? We cannot do it independently of merciful spirit.

But make no mistake – we are not born envious, greedy and hateful. Not until merciful spirit infuses our hearts are we liable to resist, to rebel and revolt, hatefully, enviously and greedily. But these are unconscious reactions. We know not what we do. Then we learn. We become aware of how our hearts, and we in our hearts, react. There comes a time, in early or later youth, when we may know the infusion of merciful spirit and then too we may learn, we may accept the teaching, that 'our' flesh is not to remain inert, a mere bondage, a mortal coil. We may learn that there is no need for us to continue to misunderstand our feelings, emotions and passions, to suppress and repress them or to be misled and waylaid by them. We are at liberty to be not only commonsensical but also compassionate.

Those who suppose they can be compassionate without being commonsensical will never get on with those who are commonsensical but do not go on to be compassionate. Western traditionalism will always be at war with eastern fundamentalism.

Compassion too has to be learned. Here the natural heart becomes aware of its incapacity for merciful spirit. Let us for the moment proceed mythologically. The natural heart sleeps and dreams. The natural head may well be awake and alert by now but the heart sleeps and dreams. The head may well know, but perhaps not enough or too much. If it knows not enough it is shocked by the heart's periodic upheavals, as it stirs in its sleep and becomes nightmarish. Insufficient understanding of the heart does not take account of the fact that merciful spirit infuses the heart too, desirous that it should wake and become aware of itself. But if the head knows too much it constructs a thorny hedge around the sleeping and dreaming heart. It wrongly supposes that the solution to problematic hate, envy and greed might lie in a killing of the heart, in a disabling of its capacity for feeling, emotion and passion.

However we have a heart of flesh and blood for good reason. That says it all for those who know and are willing to learn. We have a heart of flesh and blood for good reason.

Our limbs, are they not the extensions of our heart? The killer raises his hand against his fellow man. The coward runs from his enemy. The intellectual, the mere head, lifts not a finger to assist his fellow man.

Mythologically *and* historically speaking now, we are wrong to suppose that there ever was a time when merciful spirit did not influence head and heart. Alas, the infusion was not always possible. Note the difference between influence and infusion. One had to come who learned mercy. One had to come, to be born, I mean, who would learn and then teach mercy. Compassion as such was not until then known to mankind. Is that not a revolutionary statement? Certainly the teaching of mercy at that time was revolutionary throughout. We need not be grateful to that one but it helps. Believe me, it helps. True compassion allows us to rise as fully fledged human beings. What if we were never to countenance that we are also flesh and blood? What if we were to continue in our knowledge of ourselves as sensible people, as reasonable human beings with stiff necks and hearts of flint? The stiff neck is only an extension of the hard heart. What if we never learned true compassion? Would life be worth living? Because, still historically speaking, merciful spirit no longer just influences us. The heart is being contacted too. There is constant infusion and if we do not accept this but insist on influence alone, on a religion and science of the head, on mere head culture, we are no better off than those who know nothing, and strive for a culture of the heart alone, so that hatred, envy and greed thrive under the mask of fundamentalist faith, animal affection and brutish fondness. When the passions are released in the name of divinity, how is this essentially different

61

from when the senses are indulged in the name of market forces? False gods are false gods though no two look exactly the same.

*

The question: How does our body compare to our flesh is the same as the question: How does our compassion compare to our common sense.

Feelings, emotions and passions are carnal, are flesh and we have not yet owned them, not yet taken responsibility for them. Feeling, emotion and passion are indeed our flesh, for we have taken them up – and they have been taken up – in the resurrection process.

We cannot even imagine how this taking-up and being-taken-up in the resurrection process works if we are not knowledgeable. Our senses must be intact. Vision must be unimpaired, our eye clear. Reflection and insight are crucial for they prepare us – and through them we prepare – for the carnal process that leads into the resurrection process. Imagination sustains us meanwhile.

Our ability to discern irresponsible flesh from our own flesh, to distinguish between our flesh and our body and thirdly, to differentiate between our body, which is new, and the old body, which is indistinguishable from flesh, depends on infused merciful spirit which we love and for which we are grateful. Historic insight, which allows us to recognize infused merciful spirit in comparison to influential merciful spirit is again not of the essence, though it helps sharpen our contemporary sense of duty – of mission, if you like.

Finally we are wise to keep in mind this tendency in ourselves for head and heart to part company. We do well therefore to aim not only for creativity, but for ethical creativity. We cannot really and truly do good unless we are in the possession of both our body and our flesh. This is hardly surprising when you consider that merciful good spirit infuses both body and flesh, both head and heart, both common sense and compassion. The good we do is always ethical and communal. We cannot exclusively do ourselves good, I myself or you yourself.

*

4

How do we use or abuse our body and can we own our flesh?

We come now to the fourth question, where we inquire as to use, lack of use or insufficient use of our body, which in turn should reveal to us the nature of the abuse which highlights for us at least the possibility of 'owned flesh'; of tractable carnality.

Use and abuse of 'the flesh', mythologically speaking, are in the end one and the same. Only that making use of flesh is an abuse of our body, this brings us more narrowly to the truth of the matter.

Initially, of course, we 'use' flesh, and indulge in that sort of abuse because we know no better. A simple description of progress would be: We need to use and make use of, are practically driven to it, but having no body yet, we make the flesh do. This painfully rebounds on us. The pain makes us stand back and take notice.

How does it come we are ever so civilized and inwardly in worse shape than ever? The answer to this perfectly sensible question usually has to do with a change of foundation, a rebirth of sorts. After years or centuries of attempting to subdue the outside world and subject 'others' to our beliefs, to our convictions and whims, we come to our senses. This is true progress. We realize what it means to 'own one's body', to have a body to speak of, compared to that previous subjection to demonic flesh. So we build, we construct, we utilize. We explore and exploit. Naturally we prosper – within limits, to a point. Our culture is a head culture. We are a reasonable people and define rationality as voluntary submission to reason. We bear 'the white man's burden' honourably, highly moral and with a finely developed sense of duty.

But chaos breaks in on us. It breaks out and in on us. Oh dear, what to do! We resort to force when moral persuasion leads to impotence. When the child misbehaves (becomes unreasonable, irrational) we remove his privileges or beat him. Fear makes him obey. Except that this is a travesty of obedience. We do the same to other tribes, other peoples, other nations. Obedience based on fear instilled by force turns into rebellion and revolt. The head cannot conquer the heart by force. We experience impotence. Where have we gone wrong? Where are we going wrong? Once again pain causes us to reflect. This is a different sort of pain, but pain nonetheless. We return to the drawing board. We cannot renege on our capital promises because they make good sense. Some are bound to condemn our creativity so far but we know it makes good sense, so the fault must lie in the investment.

Let's recall how we behaved when our reasonable sovereignty was challenged – by chaos. What good sense did we make of the disorder that threatened our 'rational' order? How did we respond to the challenge of 'the flesh'? Or did we perhaps not respond at all, but merely react? Did we act out of fear in defense of our reasonable arrangements? Sounds familiar, doesn't it. Instead of re-acting fearfully might we not have responded reasona-bly? Why, when the 'others' arrived, were we right away the human beings and they the barbarians? Well then, did we deal reasonably and creatively with those barbarians? They refused to listen. It was us or them. Where partial common sense reigned for a while, total chaos ensues. Hardened hearts and stiff necks on one side, demoralized hearts and bowed necks on the other. Two sides. Not two sides of the same coin but just two sides, both of them one-sided.

Which way progress? We are surely familiar enough with our creative and commonsensical head and body. The heart however, the flesh, chaotic or forced into fearful submission, remains unfamiliar territory. The heart is actually 'the enemy'. Not *our* hear, but *the* heart. Not *our* flesh, but *the* flesh.

Our impotence, in the face of resistance, rebellion and revolt, is driven home to us. Our will to 'power' is strong as ever. Our lot is not to be envied. We thought we had it made. Then we were undone.

It must occur to us that we have been abusive. We tried to make use of the flesh. Our ambition was to har-ness the heart. Feelings, emotions and passions we pressed into service. Why abuse rather than nothing? Because of the will to power, to be ethically creative, to do good. Merciful good spirit does not give up on us just because we have taken a breather at the halfway mark and are liable to turn back. Why abuse rather than use? Because we have not yet discovered how to extend physical creativity in terms of the flesh, and so we make use of flesh, which by definition is an abusive activity.

It's hardly surprising, I suppose, that once we know to employ our senses so successfully we should also try to employ our feelings, emotions and passions when they come along. I feel happy. The world is my oyster. A despondent mood makes itself felt. This despondency shall strengthen my resolve. The supply of pearls runs out. What now? I am chairman of the Management Council. The meeting runs like clockwork. Someone steps over the traces, I call him to order, to no avail. I shout him down, I look foolish. What now? I am the president of the United Stats of America. My ideology is liberty. I bring liberty to other countries as long as they use their liberty to fill my coffers. They rebel. What now?

The nature of the abuse is an abuse of nature. It is forceful, mechanical and magical. Those who are involved in the abuse up to their necks see nothing wrong with that. Without putting too fine a point on it, let's know them, and pity them, as heartless creatures. Hatred, envy and greed fuel their activities. True enough, they are wrecking the joint, but are we to hate them for it? Are we to force them to stop? Do you suppose we might trick them into self-realization by wowing them with our charisma? Besides, how long since we ourselves behaved like that? We condemn envy because we at the moment are not envious. – but greedy. We condemn greed because at the moment we are not greedy – but hateful. We use magic to combat force, force to combat the machine, the machine to combat magic. Does that make good sense? Are we not becoming disembodied? Does our body not register the abuse?

Impotence strikes us quite rightly as a terrible predicament. Self-interest is abusive whoever pursues it, an individual, a group, a tribe or a political state. A stroke, a heart attack, societal dissolution, tribal disaffection, political malaise – they set in suddenly, they remind us of the fact that the flesh as we know and abuse it is not, or not yet, tractable. Yet we sense that it might be and so we struggle on. We refuse to believe that 'our' heart will not listen to reason. Hope springs eternal. There might be more to love than we had so far imagined. We have risen out of enslavement and know what it means to be of service. Why should we not, in spite of all our setbacks eventually become sons and daughters? Doesn't it all depend on how long we are allowed by circumstances to get away with abuse – mostly subconscious abuse?

Impotence after a taste of power, of good usefulness – it seems like such a god-awful rejection. Where is our reward for service rendered? Let's assume that a lust for might has not yet taken hold of us; that we have not yet become addicted to the use of force. Are we like the prisoner, and when the gate is opened for us we don't know where to go?

If merciful good spirit has instilled in us a will to power, to be ethically creative, then a sudden experience of impotence can mean only one thing? We are on the threshold of realization. What we do next will either mask our impotence or open us to the teaching we require.

*

5

This brings us to the last of the five questions we posed: **How does carnal pain relate to our flesh?**

The assumption here, of course, is that our flesh cannot be hurt or harmed and that we ourselves cannot be hurt or harmed via our flesh. The flesh we own is spiritualized and the spirit involved, incarnately, is merciful good spirit. Flesh can be possessed by any one or more of a legion of spirits, but when we ourselves possess it, merciful good spirit is involved, since that spirit alone, being responsible for our creation, also supports our individual and authentic creativity. Flesh possessed by an evil spirit obsesses us, which is quite a different story, because in that case our creativity is either non-ethical or it does not exist, having ceded pride of place to destructive and seductive forces and mechanisms.

Carnal pain is always a sign of physical abuse. We have to look to how we use our body and mind. In this essay we have limited ourselves to a consideration of our body. It is all the same whether we say that we abuse our body or that we use our body abusively. Our body is not, after all, a tool or an instrument, nor is it an object or a thing.

The narrow definition of words is not our object here. What we are after is practical results. The illusion

68

of progress is not actual progress. Momentarily we suppose we have succeeded, then some event catches us out and back we go to our previous state of being.

Misery is carnal pain. But our misery is always in some sense local. We speak of misery of the heart and of the soul, but a diseased tooth or an infected bladder causes us misery. She no longer loves me, so I am miserable. There is always a cause and how quickly we look for it because then we might bring our misery to a stop. A course of penicillin can deal with the misery due to the deceased tooth. Someone else loves me and the misery of my heart is allayed.

Merciful good spirit infuses my entire being. That is a fact. Never is there a moment in the life of a human being when merciful good spirit does not infuse his or her entire being. What is that human being's response?

Well, there is the initial stimulus, the impulse, rather, to make and do, to act and be busy. We feel moved to impress ourselves upon the world. Then there is the desire to know, to inspect and enquire, to understand. Then comes the question: Why bother? Who am I doing this for? I don't want to be stuck in myself alone.

The ethical impulse is awakened. I want others to know what I find out, so that they can make use of it. I am touched by their misery and there must be a reason for that. I say to them: Why don't you know what I know; after all it's there for everyone to know? And why don't you do as I do? It works, you know.

Ah, they say, it may work for you but it doesn't work for me. My misery so far is such that I cannot make head or tail of it. Help me.

But I've tried to help you, I reply. Haven't I told you what to know and what to do? But you don't do it. You are being obstinate. Secretly you don't want to be helped. My guess is that you are fond of your misery. I have nothing but contempt for you.

So that is where the relationship ends. I have tried my best. But have I? I wonder. I have known, I have done and I have shown my willingness to share the fruits of my knowledge and action. If someone rejects these, am I not bound to disregard his misery?

I might make a difference between saying: You don't accept my help, so you deserve your misery and saying: It seems I can't help you but I wish I could.

This wish nevertheless to be able to help is important, perhaps even crucial. On one hand I am aware of the misery and touched by it – by which I mean emotionally touched – and on the other hand I realize that after having given it my best shot I can do nothing about it – so far, but I am willing to learn.

This willingness to learn, in such a situation, is certainly worth mentioning. What is forestalled in this way is contempt for the one who seems to reject our help. It arises automatically, this contempt, we don't even have to instigate it. And of course it is hardening of the heart. The head is saying I have come to the end of my tether and the heart says what do you expect me to do about it? So we have to intervene.

We have to come up, as soon as possible, with a good activity of the heart. Carnal pain makes that possible for us. What, we must ask ourselves, is our final, bottom of the line attitude to misery. First of all, are we open or closed to it? Are we willing to countenance it? I mean someone else's misery now, not our own. Because what I'm going to suggest is that the best way of dealing with our own misery is to consider the misery of others. Nothing revolutionary about that thought. Then why does it appear right here, right now? Because the great misery that projects its shadow over all our being and doing is, after all, a function of our carnal mortality. The way of all flesh, that is the miserable theme. Why can we not just accept that our passage on earth is ringed round with furies? What is this mad insistence on survival?

A merciful predisposition aims its spear directly at the human heart. We wake up one morning and find ourselves confronted by a myriad expectant faces belonging to brothers and sisters, enough said. They want to know why they are miserable and what are we going to do about it. We have the explanation, as always, readily to hand but it cuts no ice. What is needed, obviously, is an example of the goods. We are creatures of the flesh, they say, and we have gathered here to spy on you. You may call us your public. We want something only you can give but we don't know what it is.

Well I'll be! A merciful predisposition, eh? So how am I, or anyone else for that matter, supposed to come up with that? Let me see now. Am I not mortal too? Am I not, like they, a creature of the flesh? Are we not all in the same boat? Sailing to where?

Not a single one of us who has not come, or will not come, to that point in time when nothing else is to be done. Our hands are empty, the larder is empty, our mind is empty. It's quite true, we stare into empty space and cannot think of a thing to do or say. Energy is ebbing, desire has gone flat, our view of ourselves is of someone marooned on a desert island and the sea is rising.

What is being demonstrated to us is the sheer uselessness of the flesh. We cannot rely on it to fuel an ambition. Simply to be, that still 'works', but not among others. They expect this and that from us and we can count on it that if we don't make at least a show of at least wishing to satisfy them they will make us uncomfortable. *It just happens*. No one can explain it. No one can justify it. But when it happens you may know you are onto a good thing.

Whatever you do now, don't throw yourself into a frenzy of activity. The temptation to do so is great. When activity is indulged in, for no other reason than to fill a terrible gap where panic sleeps and tosses restlessly, the end result is always disappointing.

The ancient way out of the predicament is slaughter. It is not a real way out but it gains a bit of time. Some form of slaughter seems to be called for to escape from the threatening vacuum. Bloodletting is what counts. Zabach. When the old priests lend a hand it is tamed, is domesticated, becomes a sacrificial slaughter. Do you want an entire nation to run amok? Better that one, or no more than a few, should be slaughtered. Then let it be animals. As long as it's a holy slaughter it's not so bad.

Still, it's nothing useful. Slaughter, sacrifice, is of the flesh. The intention is purposeful, perhaps to bribe the God, but the act, let's face it, is useless. No God worth his salt waits to be bribed.

What if we were to allow ourselves to be moved by the misery of those who look to us for what they can find nowhere else and they do not know what it is? What if we were to turn away from our own experience of nothing and turn to theirs? Without doubt this would be a distinct act. It would certainly have to be learned, as a useful alternative to useless slaughter and sacrifice.

There was no hope in the country. Money was worthless. Unemployment was high. The crops were failing. The politicians were wringing their hands, the priests were mouthing their platitudes. The stock market crashed; that was the last straw. What this country needs is a war, someone said. The call was taken up. Massive call-up! Spirits rising again, armaments industry booming, the people have rediscovered their pride – as they march to the slaughter. Who is the enemy? Why, the enemy is the enemy, of course. Let every able individual march out to kill the enemy, let him do it honourably, courageously, for king and country, for the preservation of the system, for the gaining of foreign markets, and if he asks who is really the enemy, let him be court-martialed post haste.

What a different thing it is altogether to step up to the other one and say: I know how you feel, I've been there – to say this because one knows how he feels and has been there, is perhaps there right now. To say: You can't make them go away, they've come all this way for what they suppose I can give them. Tell them to sit on the ground in groups and I'll see what I can do. I had hoped to be able to get away by myself for the weekend, into the hills, to contemplate, but here they are nevertheless, you can't just send them away hungry. Watch what I'm going to do and maybe you'll learn something. I intend to have mercy on them. We'll slaughter a few loaves and a few fishes and leave it at that. It may open their eyes to what's at stake, if not now then maybe later.

When one mortal pities another on account of his mortality, we end up with something very special.

*

So is it by way of carnal pain that we remind one another of our mortality, just in case anyone in the vicinity is capable of mercy? Is there good reason for not hiding our misery?

What if we get nothing but a return of the same? That is more than likely. You think you are having a bad time? Wait till you hear what I have to go through! Before long we all end up in an even bigger hole. In the recesses of our brain we fear what happens upon insight into abstract mortality: slaughter. We have sacrificed amply, to forestall slaughter, but total success in that direction is impossible. Maybe we should deny our mortality. Be happy. Happy people don't die, they just fade away. Eternal youth is the thing. The illusion of immortality suffices. But then nevertheless pain sets in. You are mortal, honest.

Whether we put up with our pain or manage to hide it, mercy is not involved. Mercy is crucial, if mortality is to reveal itself to us as the soft underbelly of immortality.

74

How can we possibly learn to be merciful if we were taught nothing but indifference and self-control; happiness and suicide?

We *can* learn it! Habitual emphasis on survival has to be ignored. If we are to undertake this last great adventure we have to learn not to worry where our next meal will come from or where we will spend the night and instead busy ourselves with thoughts of human nature and the search for the truth of it. Our own human nature, once we have made contact, reveals to us the spirit of truthful communication. Carnal pain, while we can bear it, conducts us in the direction of our truthful human nature where the spirit of truthful communication can take hold. This sprit is our salvation. The more thoroughly we explore it, the closer we come to the experience of immortality which embraces and absolves our mortality, so that we may know it both as our link with others and as the liability, not the fate, of death.

But let's not make a thing out of pain now. Pain can be offensive. Then we do well to distance ourselves from the offence. Should we speak of 'pain within reason'? Should we distinguish between inconvenience and agony?

What matters above all else is our inward predisposition. Are we human naturally predisposed so that we may communicate truthfully? Do we realize that this is a process of learning and more learning? Learning is made up of research and practice, of reflection and application. Are we inwardly predisposed in such a way that the quality of mercy, unstrained, can enter us as true 'manna'?

*

Once we have set out to make use of the flesh, to invest our carnality, we are in for an experience of nothing. This is a terrible, and a terrifying experience. One would not wish it on anyone. On the other hand, use of the flesh is inconceivable and out of the question. As ethical human beings, therefore, we will try to make it as plain a possible that the flesh is not employable; we will describe what is bound to happen in the case of persistent or even casual use of the flesh; we will point out that slaughter, indeed any form of sacrifice, is utterly outdated and ill-advised from the start; we will try to be compassionately present for anyone whose eyes are being opened to this insight; we will be merciful, so that the one in misery will more readily transcend from the state where he tries to use the flesh, being carnal, to where he 'possesses his flesh'. The task is formidable. Is it any wonder that we look around and use any help we can get?

A mature human being is primarily here for others and only secondarily here for himself. He knows that by helping others he helps himself. The humanist is liable to say that this too is selfishness, but not so. Selfishness is when we seek our own advantage in disregard of and even to the detriment of others.

For a mature human being, his own carnal pain will always be a sign of the onset of immaturity and therefore a steppingstone to greater maturity. He will always try to overcome his misery not by blaming someone for it but by opening himself more compassionately to the misery of others.

One is always tempted to search for internal mechanisms or external agents in order to be able to prolong one's carnal obsessions. Once we have experience of merciful spirit incarnate we may try to cling to that experience. We would like to be able to say: Now I have finally made it.

Well, in a way we can say that, because we have arrived at a watershed. From now on there should really be no more falling back into attempts to make use of the flesh. However those temptations are legion, while the experience of incarnate merciful spirit is one. So along with the experience, which proves how all sacrifice is obnoxious, we cultivate the deed. We learn to do merciful work. All misery, our own included, urges us, in the light of our experience of merciful spirit, to propagate and promulgate merciful doing and being.

*

Experience of flesh as ours is knowledge of incarnate merciful spirit. Such knowledge can be used but not used up. This is worth thinking about. Using knowledge is a way of investing it. We might think of it as a sowing of seed and the seed must die before there can be the new creature. Knowledge of merciful good spirit incarnate however is not to be invested but to be contemplated, meditated upon, recollected and the like. It is, after all, the knowledge toward which all other knowledge points as its goal; its home, so to speak.

The contemplation of *our* flesh, of merciful good spirit incarnate, leads to works that make merciful good spirit available to others. Meanwhile pain cannot affect us and cannot overwhelm us. Of course we must be quite aware of that. It won't do to lose track of the workings of merciful spirit in the light of day. Pain always reminds us of a shortcoming in our awareness or a shortfall in our constitution. Both of these are measured against our merciful awareness.

In conclusion, then, our answer to the question: How does carnal pain relate to our flesh? must be: It does not relate at all. Where there is the one, the other cannot be. Neither do they mutually exclude each other, because we ourselves are the agents and we live in the one or die in the other. In the flesh we die, in our flesh we live. It comes down to a question of endurance and perseverance, of determination and discipline, of confidence and courage.

* * *   (July 2005)

Index: pg

*

79

www.ingramcontent.com/pod-product-compliance
Lightning Source LLC
Chambersburg PA
CBHW070300290526
45791CB00003B/1016